To Vanya

Violin Playtime Book 1

very first pieces with piano accompaniment

selected and edited by

Paul de Keyser

Faber Music Limited

London

To the Teacher

With *Violin Playtime*, the beginner violinist can make music from the very first lessons. In the three books that make up the series there are over a hundred little pieces, a treasure-trove of attractive tunes – some traditional, some by composers of the past, some newly composed.

But *Violin Playtime* is more than just an easy anthology; the underlying approach is 'learn as you play', and a carefully devised groundplan of technical development makes it a manual in disguise, a tutor without text.

Since there are plenty of contrasting pieces at each level, the young player is given scope to master new technical elements without tedious repetition of the same material. All the pieces in the three books are in first position, and the piano accompaniments are deliberately simple.

Book 1 takes the young violinist from the very beginning to a standard approximately equivalent to that of Associated Board (U.K.) Grade 1. It is organised in two parts: in Part One (pieces 1–36) the second finger is exclusively in its forward placement, and in Part Two (pieces 37–47) it is exclusively in its backward placement. You can thus select the route taken to suit each individual pupil.

I would like to thank Jonathan Dunsby for his superlative piano accompaniments, which make each piece an artistic miniature evoking the mood implied by its title. I am also grateful to Anna Pugh for her lively illustrations which pupils should be encouraged to colour in, perhaps while learning the appropriate piece.

Paul de Keyser

© 1986 by Faber Music Ltd
First published in 1986 by Faber Music Ltd
3 Queen Square London WC1N 3AU
Music engraved by Allan Hill
Illustrations by Anna Pugh
Cover design by M & S Tucker
Printed in England

Separate violin parts are available (U.K. only)

INDEX

Violin Playtime Book 1

PART ONE

1. The Grand Old Duke of York

TRADITIONAL

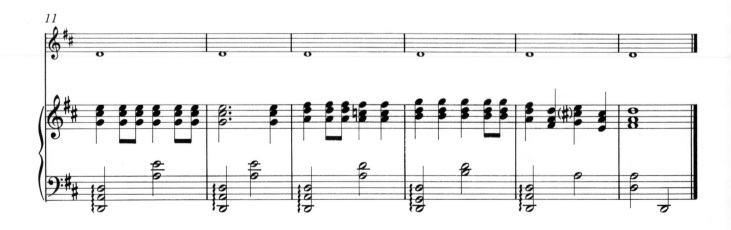

2. Sur le pont d'Avignon

FRENCH

3. The Major General

SIR ARTHUR SULLIVAN
(1842–1900)

4. Mazurka

4

5. Orientale

6. In Winter

7. Wagon Train

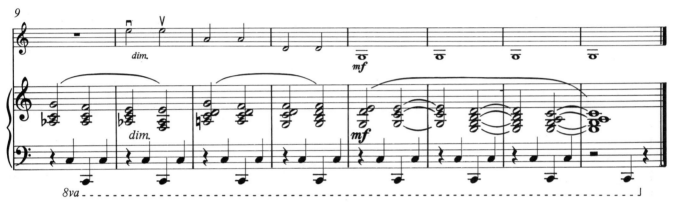

8. From D to E

9. The River

10. The Chicken Cheeps

BULGARIAN

11. Bells

12. Soldiers' March

13. In Olden Times

VALENTIN HAUSSMANN
(*c*1567–*c*1614)

14. Song without Words

BULGARIAN

15. By the Lake

16. Puppet on a String

17. Children Playing

RUSSIAN

18. Mary had a Little Lamb

TRADITIONAL

10

19. From 4th to Open

20. The Courageous Climber

21. Raindrops

22. In the Moonlight

FRENCH

23. Marche Militaire

24. Song of Sorrow

25. In the Sun

26. Round Dance

27. Gliding Along

28. The Bells of St. Basil's

14

29. Pony Trot

30. Go to Sleep

31. Old Macdonald

TRADITIONAL

32. Poème

33. The Hobby Horse

GERMAN

34. The Rainbow

35. Courtly Dance

BARTOLOMEO CAMPAGNOLI
(1751–1827)

36. Hungarian Dance

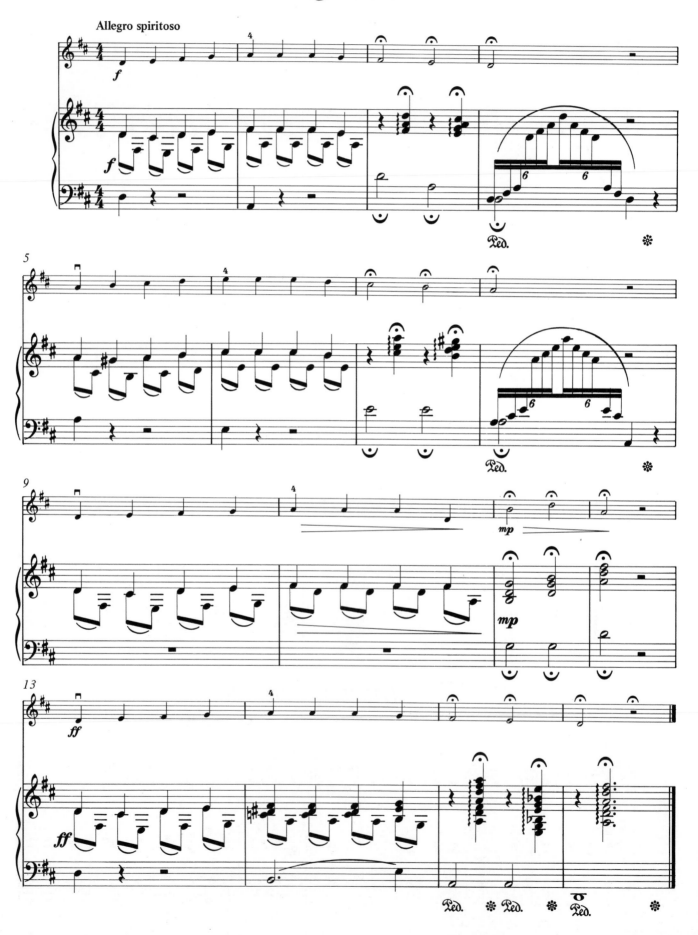

PART TWO

37. The Great Cathedral

38. Chorale

39. Lullaby

40. Welsh Winter

41. Etude

BARTOLOMEO CAMPAGNOLI
(1751–1827)

42. Nursery Rhyme

BULGARIAN

43. Andante

FERDINAND DAVID
(1810–1873)

44. The Fields of Flax

CZECH

45. Balloons in the Sky

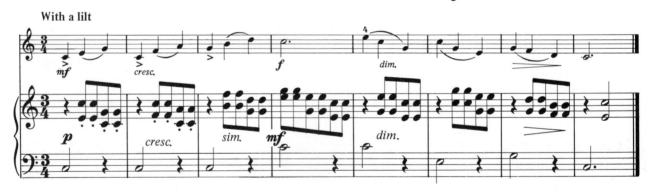

46. Hush, Little Baby

TRADITIONAL